USBORNE

Picture Atlas of EUROPE

Jonathan Melmoth

Illustrated by Brian Fitzgerald

Designed by Samantha Barrett and Freya Harrison

Cartography by Craig Asquith

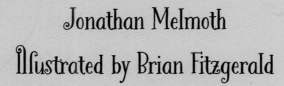

MAP 7

~- Lake Ladoga

RUSSIA

-~ Volga starts here

■ Moscow

The Ural Mountains
mark the boundary
between Europe and
Asia in Russia.

Minsk

BELARUS

MAP 8

UKRAINE

■ Kiev

Volga ends here

MOLDOVA

Mount Elbrus

Chisinau

ROMANIA

The ownership of
this area, known as
Crimea, is disputed by
Russia and Ukraine.

MAP 9

charest

Black Sea

~- BULGARIA

■ Ankara

Only this part
of Turkey is
in Europe.

TURKEY

Nicosia ■

CYPRUS

EUROPE

Europe is one of seven large areas of
land in the world, called continents. It is
made up of 47 countries and is home
to over 750 million people.

WORLD MAP

Europe

North
America

Asia

Africa

South
America

Oceania

Antarctica

ABOUT THIS ATLAS

There are ten detailed picture maps in this book.
The map of Europe on these pages shows which
countries appear on each map.

Parts of Russia and Turkey are in Europe and parts of them
are in Asia. Only the European parts are shown in this book.

Look for these symbols on each map:

■ CAPITAL CITY   Hills and mountains

● Large city   Rivers and lakes

EUROPE RECORDS

Highest mountain Mount Elbrus, Russia
5,642m (18,510ft)

Longest river Volga, Russia
3,692km (2,294 miles)

Largest lake Ladoga, Russia
17,700km² (6,834 sq. miles)

Highest waterfall Vinnufossen, Norway
860m (2,822ft)

MAP 1

REPUBLIC OF IRELAND
UNITED KINGDOM

Faroe Islands

Shetland Islands

Shetland pony

Orkney Islands

Golden eagle

Puffin

Faroe Islands
(Denmark)

Sheep

Bagpiper

Thistle

One of the Lewis Chessmen

The Lewis Chessmen are carved from walrus tusks. They were made around 800 years ago.

Hebrides

Harris tweed is a woollen cloth woven by hand in the Hebrides.

Harris tweed

Killer whale

Atlantic Ocean

Dia duit!
(pronounced 'jee-uh ditch')

Irish

The Giant's Causeway is made up of thousands of stone columns formed by an ancient volcanic eruption.

Giant's Causeway

Highland Games

Jacobite steam train

Performer at the Edinburgh Festival

SCOTLAND

Balmoral Castle

Balmoral Castle is owned by the British royal family.

Aberdeen

Golf at St Andrews

Edinburgh

Glasgow

Alnwick Castle

Oil rig

North

... Sea

The Angel of the North sculpture, Gateshead

Newcastle-upon-Tyne

Fish and chips

Norfolk Broads

London skyline

Channel Tunnel

King Harold II was killed at the Battle of Hastings in 1066.

King Harold II

UNITED KINGDOM

ENGLAND

Cambridge

LONDON

Thames

Football

Oxford

William Shakespeare

Hadrian's Wall

Manchester

Liverpool

Birmingham

Cricket

Stonehenge

Isle of Wight

Red kite

Severn

Sailing regatta

Isle of Man (UK)

Welsh dragon, a national emblem

WALES

Cardiff

Stonehenge is a monument built around 5,000 years ago.

Channel Islands (UK)

Motorcycle racing

Daffodils

Cream tea

Irish Sea

Belfast

NORTHERN IRELAND

Titanic Museum, Belfast

DUBLIN

Gulliver's Travels

Gulliver's Travels is a novel written by Dubliner, Jonathan Swift.

Hello!

English

Surfing

Penzance

Agapanthus

Isles of Scilly

REPUBLIC OF IRELAND

Shamrock, a national emblem

Shannon

Folk singers

Cork

Grey seal

Irish dancers

THE UNION FLAG

The United Kingdom is made up of four nations. The flag is a combination of three national flags.

England

Scotland

Northern Ireland

The Welsh flag isn't included because Wales was already part of the kingdom of England when the Union Flag was designed.

National flag of Wales

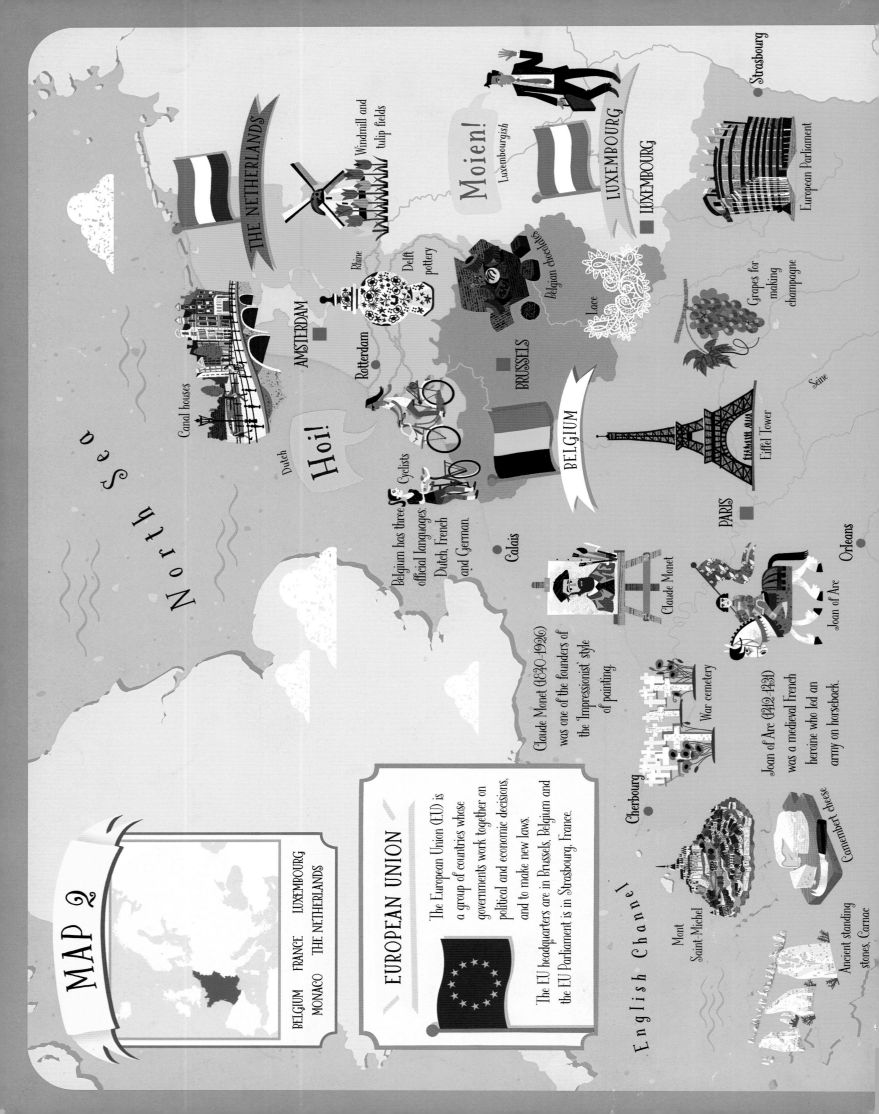

MAP 2

BELGIUM   FRANCE   LUXEMBOURG

MONACO   THE NETHERLANDS

EUROPEAN UNION

The European Union (EU) is a group of countries whose governments work together on political and economic decisions, and to make new laws.

The EU headquarters are in Brussels, Belgium and the EU Parliament is in Strasbourg, France.

North Sea

THE NETHERLANDS

Windmill and tulip fields

Rhine

Delft pottery

Canal houses

AMSTERDAM

Rotterdam

Dutch

Hoi!

Cyclists

Belgium has three official languages: Dutch, French and German.

Moien!

Luxembourgish

LUXEMBOURG

LUXEMBOURG

European Parliament

Strasbourg

Belgian chocolates

Lace

BRUSSELS

BELGIUM

Grapes for making champagne

Seine

Eiffel Tower

PARIS

Calais

Claude Monet (1840–1926) was one of the founders of the Impressionist style of painting.

Claude Monet

Joan of Arc (1412–1431) was a medieval French heroine who led an army on horseback.

Joan of Arc

Orleans

English Channel

Cherbourg

War cemetery

Mont Saint-Michel

Camembert cheese

Ancient standing stones, Carnac

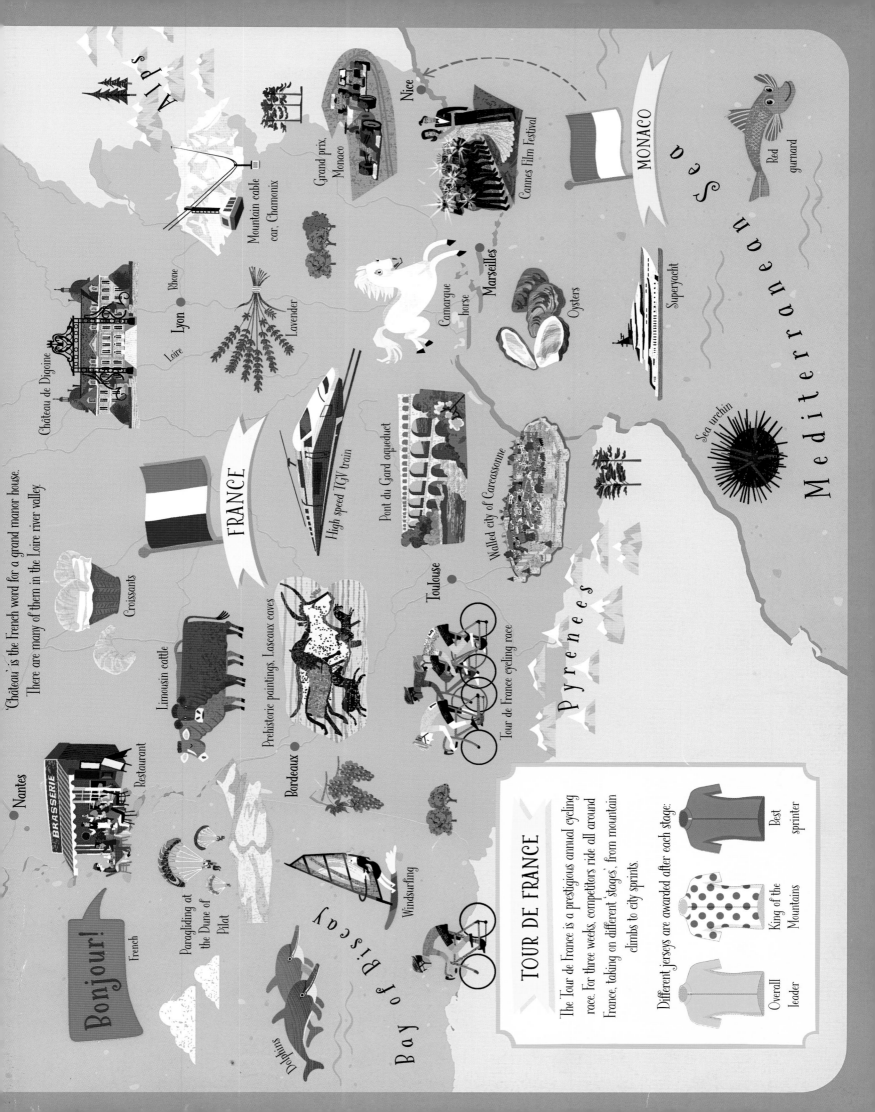

Alps

Mountain cable
car, Chamonix

Grand prix,
Monaco

Nice

Cannes Film Festival

MONACO

Mediterranean Sea

Red
gurnard

Lyon

Rhône

Loire

Lavender

Camargue
horse

Marseilles

Oysters

Superyacht

Château de Digoine

Sea urchin

FRANCE

High speed TGV train

Pont du Gard aqueduct

Walled city of Carcassonne

'Château' is the French word for a grand manor house.
There are many of them in the Loire river valley.

Croissants

Limousin cattle

Prehistoric paintings, Lascaux caves

Toulouse

Pyrenees

Nantes

Restaurant

Bordeaux

Tour de France cycling race

Bonjour!

French

Paragliding at
the Dune of
Pilat

Windsurfing

Bay of Biscay

Dolphins

TOUR DE FRANCE

The Tour de France is a prestigious annual cycling
race. For three weeks, competitors ride all around
France, taking on different 'stages', from mountain
climbs to city sprints.

Different jerseys are awarded after each stage:

Overall
leader

King of the
Mountains

Best
sprinter

Octopus

Atlantic Ocean

Sardines

Surfing

For hundreds of years pilgrims have hiked a long trail to Santiago de Compostela.

Santiago de Compostela

Pilgrims

Gijon

¡Hola!

Spanish

Classical guitar

Tapas

Barcelos rooster

Oporto

Douro

SPAIN

Royal Palace of Madrid

MADR

Olá!

Portuguese

PORTUGAL

Decorative 'azulejo' tile

Dry-cured ham

Bullfighting

Traditional pavement design

Pena National Palace

Sunflowers

Great Mosque of Cordoba

Belem Tower, Lisbon

LISBON

Cork

Oranges

Cordoba

Custard tarts

Figs

Faro

Seville

El Tajo gorge, Ronda

Gra

Algarve

Malaga

Vasco da Gama's ship

Vasco da Gama was a Portuguese explorer. In 1499 he became the first person to sail from Europe to India.

Barbary monkey, Gibraltar

Costa del Sol

Gibraltar (UK)

Guggenheim Museum,
Bilbao

ilbao

Hola!

Catalan

ANDORRA

Pyrenees

ANDORRA LA VELLA

Salvador Dali was an eccentric 20th-century artist known for his bizarre, highly imaginative paintings.

Salvador Dali

Ebro

Mountain goat

Sagrada Familia

Costa Brava

Barcelona

Human tower building competitions are popular in the area around Barcelona.

Human tower

The Sagrada Familia is an extraordinary church designed by an architect called Antoni Gaudi.

Tagus

Tomato festival, Bunol

Valencia

Fireworks display at Las Fallas festival of fire

Majorca   Minorca

Holiday villa

Balearic Islands

Mediterranean Sea

Paella

Ibiza

Paella is a traditional dish made with saffron rice and seafood.

Alicante

Costa Blanca

Beach party, Ibiza

Flamenco dancers

MAP 3

ANDORRA   PORTUGAL   SPAIN

Schönbrunn Palace

Austrian German

VIENNA

Servus!

Spanish Riding School

Danube

MAP 4

AUSTRIA   ITALY   LIECHTENSTEIN
MALTA   SAN MARINO
SWITZERLAND   VATICAN CITY

Graz

Veal schnitzel

AUSTRIA

Wolfgang Amadeus Mozart (1756–1791) wrote over 600 pieces of classical music.

Wolfgang Amadeus Mozart

Edelweiss flower

Trieste

St Mark's Basilica, Venice

Adriatic Sea

SAN MARINO

Tourists on a gondola boat

Venice

LIECHTENSTEIN

Skiing

Juliet's balcony

Statue of David

Tomatoes

SAN MARINO

Apennines

Tiber

Swiss Army knife

VADUZ

Mountain chalets

This balcony in Verona was made famous by the play, Romeo and Juliet.

Po

Florence

Leaning Tower of Pisa

A drawing by the artist and scientist Leonardo da Vinci (1452–1519)

SWITZERLAND

Zurich

Emmental cheese

Alps

Milan

Genoa

Manarola, Cinque Terre

Gruezi!

Swiss German

Geneva

BERN

Alphorn player

Fashion model

Turin

Mole Antonelliana, a museum in Turin

Napoléon Bonaparte (1769–1821) was born on Corsica. He became a military leader who won many victories and made himself emperor of France.

Corsica (France)

Sports car

Napoléon Bonaparte

Ice cream

Trulli houses

Yacht

Merħba!
Maltese

ITALY

Pizza

Espresso coffee

Mount Etna

MALTA

Colosseum
in Rome

Naples

Ruins of Pompeii

The city of Pompeii was destroyed
by a volcanic eruption in the year
79. The ash from the eruption
preserved many objects, which you
can still see today.

ROME

Roman soldier

2,000 years ago, the
Romans ruled a vast empire
from their capital, Rome.

Opera house, Palermo

Sicily

VALLETTA

VATICAN CITY
Vatican City is a religious
city state within Rome.

Ciao!
(pronounced 'chow')
Italian

Palermo

Lemons

M e d i t e r r a n e a n   S e a

T y r r h e n i a n   S e a

Snorkelling

Speedboat

Wild boar

Sardinia

Beach
holiday

Cruise ship

PASTA

Pasta is a traditional Italian food made from flour
mixed with egg or water. It can be made in many
different shapes:

Farfalle

Fusilli

Spaghetti

N o r t h   S e a

Wadden Sea nature reserve

Port of Hamburg

● Hamburg

'Wurst' sausage

Kingfisher

Elbe

Bremen
●

Car factory

Brandenburg Gate,
Berlin

BERLIN ■

Garden
gnome

Fans of the football club Borussia
Dortmund make spectacular
displays at matches.
Dortmund football fans

Dortmund ●

Hansel and Gretel,
a German fairy tale

Hallo!
German

Martin Luther (1483-1546),
a religious reformer

Cologne Cathedral

Rhine

Red
squirrel

Cologne ●

20 Euro note

The European Central
Bank is in Frankfurt.

GERMANY

This medieval clock
displays the location of
stars and planets, as
well as telling the time.

Astronomical clock, Prague

● Frankfurt

Christmas market, Nuremberg

PRAGUE ■

Gutenberg
printing press

The printing press using metal
type was invented by Frankfurter
Johannes Gutenberg in 1439.

Stuttgart ●

$E = mc^2$
$\mu = \dfrac{E_0}{V^2}$
$R_{\mu\nu} = 0$

Albert Einstein
(1879-1955), a
brilliant physicist

Danube

CZECH REPUBLIC

Black Forest
gateau

Munich ●

Pretzel

Neuschwanstein
Castle

Gingerbread heart
Ich liebe dich

Traditional breeches
called 'Lederhosen'

Baltic Sea

Cześć!
Polish

Gdansk

Malbork Castle

Masurian Lake District

European bison

Dancing the Polonaise

Nicolaus Copernicus (1473-1543), an astronomer

Vistula

POLAND

Castle Square, Warsaw

Poznan

Oder

Pickled cucumbers

Frédéric Chopin (1810-1849), a pianist and composer

Traditional embroidery pattern

WARSAW

Wild mushrooms

Wroclaw

Painted townhouses

Auschwitz is a former prison camp which is now a museum and memorial to the people who were killed there by the Nazis during the Second World War.

Coat of arms of Poland

This chapel is carved out of rock salt deep underground at Wieliczka salt mine.

Auschwitz

Krakow

Wieliczka salt mine

The word for 'hello' is the same in the Czech and Slovak languages.

Ahoj!

Carpathian Mountains

Tatra chamois

Kosice

MAP 5

White-water rafting

Czech folk music group

SLOVAKIA

BRATISLAVA

Bratislava Castle

CZECH REPUBLIC   GERMANY
POLAND   SLOVAKIA

Barents Sea

The Northern Lights are spectacular natural light displays in the night sky.

The Sami people have lived in northern Scandinavia for at least the last 5,000 years.

Sami people

Reindeer

Finnish

Hei!

Cross-country skiing

FINLAND

Oulu

Northern lights

Nordic patterned sweater

This tourist attraction claims to be the home of Santa Claus.

Santa Claus Village, Lapland

Smörgåsbord meal

Gulf of Bothnia

Luleå

Blueberries

Kiruna

SWEDEN

Traditional log house

Umeå

Norwegian

Hallo!

Ice climbing

Husky dog sledding

ICELAND

Arctic fox

Vatna Glacier

Atlantic Ocean

Norwegian Sea

NORWAY

Fishing

Hallo!

Icelandic

The Great Geysir

Turf roofed house

REYKJAVIK

Leif Erikson

The explorer Leif Erikson was the first European to reach America around 1,000 years ago.

MAP 6

DENMARK   ESTONIA   FINLAND
ICELAND   LATVIA   LITHUANIA
NORWAY   RUSSIA   SWEDEN

Iceland

Viking longboat

MAP 7

RUSSIA (northern)

Murmansk

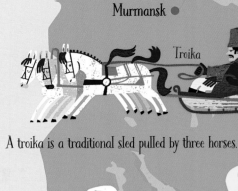

A troika is a traditional sled pulled by three horses.

Troika

Icebreaker

Russian words are written in the Cyrillic alphabet.

ЗАРАВСТВУЙТЕ!
(pronounced 'zdravst-vuy-tye')

Russian

Orthodox priest

Tundra swan

W h i t e   S e a

Dill

Arkhangelsk

For hundreds of years, Russia was ruled by all-powerful monarchs called Tsars. Tsar Peter the Great, founded St. Petersburg in 1703.

Peter the Great

Wooden church, Kizhi

Plesetsk spaceport

Northern Dvina

These priceless egg-shaped ornaments are encrusted with precious jewels.

Honey

Fabergé egg

Lake Ladoga

St. Petersburg

RUSSIA

Ballet dancer

The Catherine Palace

Walled city of Velikii Novgorod

Cherepovets

Leo Tolstoy (1828-1910) wrote the classic novel, *War and Peace.*

White-backed woodpecker

Tver

St. Basil's Cathedral, Moscow

Leo Tolstoy

Yuri Gagarin (1934-1968) became the first man in space in 1961.

MOSCOW

Smolensk

Yuri Gagarin

Barents Sea

THE SOVIET UNION

In 1917, a workers' group called the Bolsheviks seized control of Russia in a violent revolution.

They created a powerful new state called the Soviet Union, which included Russia and many other countries in the former Russian empire.

In 1991, the Soviet Union collapsed and Russia became a separate country once again. Today, it is governed by an elected president.

Polar bear

Vast forests cover much of this part of Russia.

Traditional wooden handicrafts

Ob

Snowflakes

Wolverine

Lynx

Ukhta

EUROPE

ASIA

Snowmobile

Winter is very cold in Russia. Temperatures can drop as low as -45°C (-49°F).

Matryoshka dolls

The Ural Mountains mark the eastern edge of Europe. Beyond them, the rest of Russia is in Asia.

Oil pipelines

Wolf

Cranberries

Ice hockey

Ural Mountains

The Trans-Siberian Railway is the longest in the world. It stretches over 9,000km (5,700 miles) from Moscow to Vladivostok, in the far east of Russia.

Kirov

Perm

A trolleybus is an electric bus which draws power from overhead lines.

Trans-Siberian Railway

Kazan mosque

Volga

Kazan

Kama

Trolleybus

SOUTHERN RUSSIA

Brown bear

Wooden 'dacha' holiday house

Прывітанне!
(pronounced 'privitanye')
Belarusian

MOSCOW

NORTHERN
RUSSIA

Vitsyebsk

Smolensk

Tractor

BELARUS

Elk

MINSK

Camomile flowers

Railway museum, Brest

Mir Castle

Homyel

Kursk

Вітаю!
(pronounced 'vitayoo')
Ukrainian

Ukraine is nicknamed
'the breadbasket of
Europe' because many
crops grow there, such
as wheat.

The six-engine Antonov An-225
is the largest plane ever built.

Wheat

Monastery of the Caves, Kiev

Cossack Mamay is a
mythical hero, celebrated for
his strength and courage.

Cossack Mamay

Kharkiv

Antonov
An-225

KIEV

Stork

Borshch soup

Dnieper

Salut!
Moldovan

A people's uprising took place
on these stairs in 1905.

UKRAINE

Traditional dancers

Askania-Nova nature reserve

Potemkin Stairs

CHISINAU

Odessa

MOLDOVA

The ownership of
this area, known as
Crimea, is disputed by
Ukraine and Russia.

Swallow's
Nest castle

Sevastopol

B l a c k   S e a

Ryazan

Tea samovar

Potatoes

Ulyanovsk

Zhiguli dam

MAP 8

BELARUS   MOLDOVA
RUSSIA (southern)   UKRAINE

Cherries

River cruise ship

RUSSIA

Saratov

Voronezh

Russian Rouble coins

Balalaika

The Motherland Calls', Volgograd

This huge statue commemorates the terrible Battle of Stalingrad in the Second World War. Stalingrad has since been renamed Volgograd.

Volga

Don

Steel factory

Volgograd

Astrakhan kremlin, a fortress in the heart of the city

Dalmatian pelican

Cabbage field

Donetsk

Golden Temple, Kalmykia

Astrakhan

C a s p i a n   S e a

Rostov-on-Don

Many people in the Kalmykia region follow the Buddhist religion.

Lotus flower

Caspian seals

The Caspian Sea is actually a lake – the largest in the world.

Musical fountains, Krasnodar

Mikhail Lermontov (1814–1841) was a great poet, killed in a duel at the age of 26.

Mikhail Lermontov

Krasnodar

Caviar

Mount Elbrus is the highest mountain in Europe. It is 5,642m (18,510ft) tall.

Grozny

Snowboarding

Sochi

Mount Elbrus

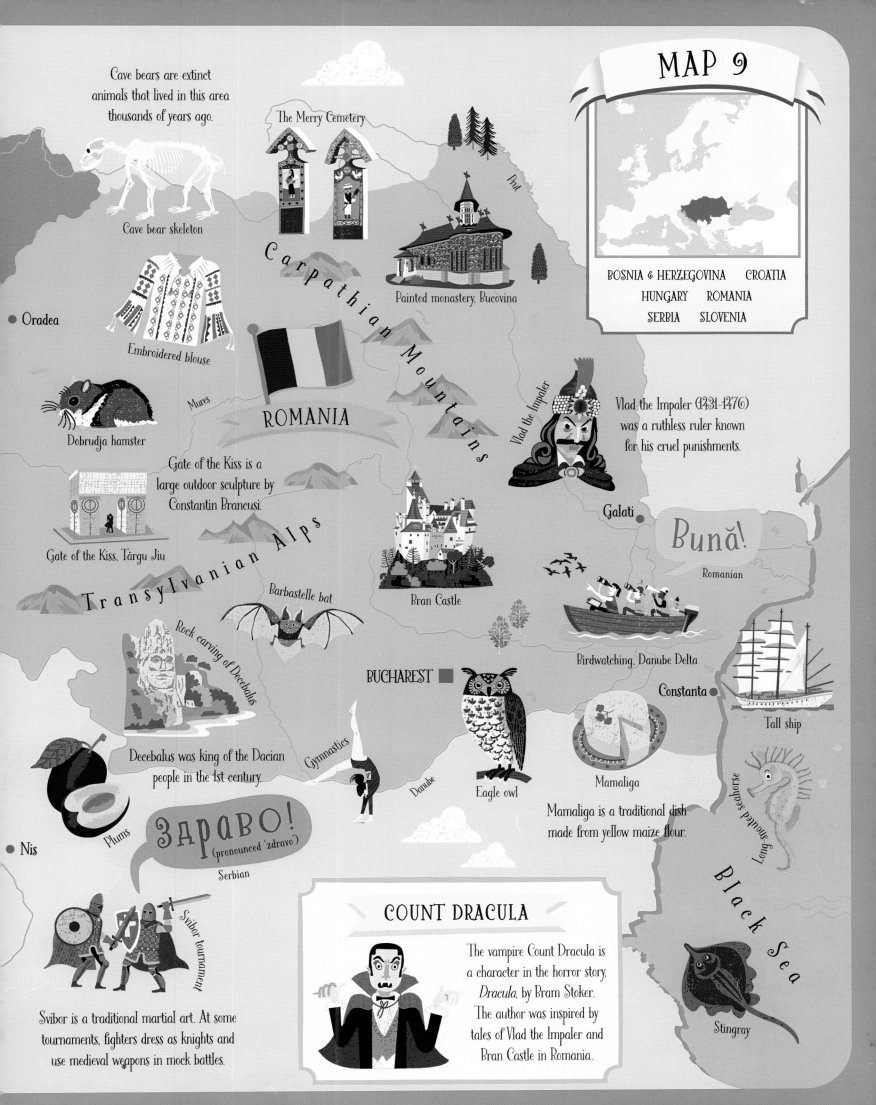

Cave bears are extinct animals that lived in this area thousands of years ago.

Cave bear skeleton

The Merry Cemetery

Prut

Painted monastery, Bucovina

MAP 9

BOSNIA & HERZEGOVINA   CROATIA
HUNGARY   ROMANIA
SERBIA   SLOVENIA

Carpathian Mountains

Oradea

Embroidered blouse

ROMANIA

Mures

Dobrudja hamster

Gate of the Kiss is a large outdoor sculpture by Constantin Brancusi.

Gate of the Kiss, Târgu Jiu

Transylvanian Alps

Vlad the Impaler

Vlad the Impaler (1231-1476) was a ruthless ruler known for his cruel punishments.

Galati

Buna!

Romanian

Bran Castle

Rock carving of Decebalus

Barbastelle bat

Birdwatching, Danube Delta

Constanta

Tall ship

Decebalus was king of the Dacian people in the 1st century.

Gymnastics

BUCHAREST

Danube

Eagle owl

Mamaliga

Mamaliga is a traditional dish made from yellow maize flour.

Long snouted seahorse

Plums

ЗДРАВО!
(pronounced 'zdravo')

Serbian

Nis

Black Sea

Svibor tournament

COUNT DRACULA

The vampire Count Dracula is a character in the horror story, *Dracula*, by Bram Stoker. The author was inspired by tales of Vlad the Impaler and Bran Castle in Romania.

Stingray

Svibor is a traditional martial art. At some tournaments, fighters dress as knights and use medieval weapons in mock battles.

MAP 10

ALBANIA   BULGARIA   CYPRUS
GREECE   KOSOVO   MACEDONIA
MONTENEGRO   TURKEY

Cyprus

Black Sea

Harbour porpoise

Gold artifacts found in Varna date back over 6,500 years. They are the oldest ever found.

Gold treasure from Varna

Varna

Bulgarian

ЗДРАВЕЙ!
(pronounced 'zdravei')

Kaval, a Bulgarian flute

Accordion

Danube

The official languages of Kosovo are Albanian and Serbian.

Hare

Macedonian

ЗДРАВО!
(pronounced 'zdravo')

KOSOVO

PRISTINA ■

Montenegrin

Zdravo!

MONTENEGRO

PODGORICA ■

Porto Montenegro marina

Opinga shoes

Albanian

Tungjatjeta!
(pronounced 'tung'yat-yeta')

ALBANIA

TIRANA ■

Korçë ●

Çifteli, a traditional stringed instrument

Roses

BULGARIA

Alexander Nevsky Cathedral, Sofia

● SOFIA

To celebrate the start of spring, people tie red and white decorations called 'martenitsi' on trees

Martenitsa tree

Over 2,000 years ago, Alexander the Great of Macedonia conquered an empire stretching all the way to India.

Alexander the Great

MACEDONIA

SKOPJE ■

6th-century mosaic

Thessaloniki ●

Larisa ●

Greek rock lizard

Corfu

The Blue Mosque, Istanbul

Istanbul ●

Turkish

Merhaba!

Spice market

Sea of Marmara

Only a small part of Turkey is in Europe. The part east of the Sea of Marmara is in Asia.

Aegean Sea

Ancient pottery

TURKEY

The capital of Turkey, Ankara, is in the Asian part of the country.

Butterflies

Ruins of the Palace of Knossos

CYPRUS

NICOSIA

Scuba diving

Limassol

Waterpark

In Cyprus, the official languages are Greek and Turkish.

Rhodes

Dodecanese Islands

Windmill

Whitewashed buildings

Irakleio

Crete

Cyclades Islands

GREECE

Plate smashing

Loggerhead sea turtle

ATHENS

Parthenon temple, Athens

Ancient Spartan soldier

Spartan soldiers were famous for their skill and bravery.

Γεια!
(pronounced 'ya')
Greek

Smashing plates is a tradition at Greek weddings.

Greek salad

Olympia

Kalamata

Olympic Games

Squid

Ionian Islands

The first Olympic Games were held at Olympia nearly 3,000 years ago.

Shrimps

Starfish

Sea sponge

Mediterranean Sea

GREEK MYTHS

Greek myths are ancient stories which tell of courageous heroes, fierce gods and hideous monsters. Here are characters from some of the most famous ones:

Perseus and Medusa

Theseus and the Minotaur

Pandora with her box

EUROPE QUIZ

Test your knowledge with these ten questions about Europe.
Look back through the book to find the answers, and check them below.

1. Which country has this flag?

What are the names of these famous landmarks?

2. A castle in Romania

3. A cathedral in Russia

4. A sculpture in the UK

5. In which country would you find Camargue horses?

6. How do you say 'hello' in Turkish?

7. In which country is paella a traditional dish?

8. What's the capital of Poland?

9. Where would you find these cone-shaped trulli houses?

10. What's the name of this famous Icelandic explorer?

Answers: 1. Belarus, 2. Bran Castle, 3. St. Basil's Cathedral, 4. The Angel of the North, 5. France, 6. Merhaba, 7. Spain, 8. Warsaw, 9. Italy, 10. Leif Erikson

INTERNET LINKS

For links to websites where you can find out more about places, people and animals around Europe, go to Usborne Quicklinks at www.usborne.co.uk/quicklinks and type in 'Atlas of Europe'.

Edited by Ruth Brocklehurst   Series designed by Stephen Moncrieff

First published in 2017 by Usborne Publishing Ltd., 83-85 Saffron Hill, London, EC1N 8RT, England. www.usborne.com. Copyright © 2017 Usborne Publishing Ltd.

INDEX